GLASS STONE ART

Project Book

Learn how to create a collection of amazing glass stones.

5 projects inside

INTRODUCTION

Welcome to the wonderful world of Glass Stone Art!

This kit is designed specifically for adults only.

Learning a new skill is always exciting – we're here to help you get started. Glass stone art is like treasure, it offers beautiful designs and fabulous moments to be with yourself and your artistic talents. Creating glass stone art allows us to free our minds and promotes relaxation. Your glass stone art can be decorative and inspirational, or you can create gifts for family and friends. The possibilities are endless, particularly with the wide variety of mediums that can be used, including papercraft, glitter, paints, text, and much more!

From creating affirmation positivity stones to the alphabet, there is something that will appeal to you. You could take a positive affirmation that will inspire you or give you strength. Write it on your stone with a permanent marker, before decorating it with nail varnish or glitter glue. Place your stone somewhere that you will see it so you can be reminded of the positive message.

Let's get your creativity flowing and open your mind to this new and unlimited world. This kit provides everything you need to make your very own decorative glass stone art. There are also four other options, each with a step-by-step guide for you to try. Remember, every skill takes effort to master, so don't be disheartened if it's not perfect the first time. The most important thing is that you have fun and enjoy yourself.

Let's start your glass stone art journey!

KIT CONTENTS

WHAT'S INCLUDED:

· 2x Large glass stones
· 3x Small glass stones
· 5x Decorative papers
· 20ml Craft glue
· White felt backing sheet

WHAT YOU'LL NEED:

·Craft scissors
·Paint brush (optional)
·Dry, soft cloth

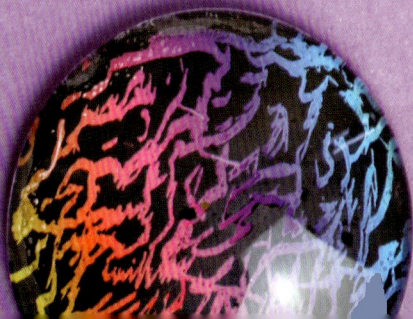

GETTING STARTED

There is much more to glass stone art than just glass stones! They have many uses, from decorating to gifting. See a list of ideas below:

· As part of a treasure box for a loved one
· As decoration for card making
· Fridge magnets
· A friendship gift
· Home decor
· Positivity stones
· Seasonal fun gifts and decorations
· Paper weights
· Jewellery
· Wall art
· Jar decoration with fairy lights
· Alphabet learning tool for children
· Wedding favours or decoration

DIFFERENT TECHNIQUES AND MEDIUMS

This project book will demonstrate five different methods for creating these fantastic glass stones.There are endless mediums that you can use, we have listed a few below:

· Paper/backing card - maps, books, dictionaries /words, star signs, stars, magazine cuttings, playing cards - you can use a varied thickness for your paper and card.

· Foil paper – sticking foiling paper or gold leaf foil for a sophisticated décor.

· Mandalas – dotting paint in repetitive patterns.

· Animal stone art – fun and playful animals, insects, and bugs.

· Glitter glue – sparkly and decorative.

· Pens – using an array of permanent pens are always an easier option!

· Hand painted – if you are more of an artist, why not paint intricate scenes or portraits?

· Alcohol ink – create abstract art by using alcohol inks to make a marbling effect.

· Nail varnish – marbling, painting abstract patterns.

· Photography - family photos/portraits or abstract/modern texture and macro shots or flowers and nature!

FACT!

Glass Stones, also known as Cabochon from Middle French caboche, meaning head, is a gemstone that has been shaped and polished, as opposed to faceted. The resulting form is usually a convex (rounded) obverse with a flat reverse. Cabochon was the default method of preparing gemstones before gemstone cutting was developed.

These dome shaped glass stones can be purchased at most craft stores in various shapes and sizes, and are a really creative way to display and magnify all types of art.

WARNINGS!

All the makes included in this book are designed specifically for adults.

Please work in a well-ventilated room when using any solvents or glue.

As a precaution, we'd suggest working on a covered work surface and wearing protective, or old clothing in case of any spillages.

Keep all glass stones out of the reach of children and pets, as well as finished products.

RAINBOW

RAINBOW

Get cracking with these ombre rainbow glass stones. Customise your glass stones with the decorative ombre rainbow papers.

YOU WILL NEED

- Craft scissors
- Paint brush (optional)
- Soft cloth

KIT INCLUDES

- 2x Large glass stones
- 3x Small glass stones
- 20ml Craft glue
- Crafting felt

METHOD

1. Make sure you're working on a clean and spacious work surface; this is all part of the mindfulness and enjoyment of glass stone craft. Once ready, empty the contents of the box onto the surface and give each stone a wipe over with a soft, dry cloth.

2. Position the first of your larger stones over the desired area of where you want to magnify. Ensure your preferred colours are showing through.

3. When you are happy with the positioning, apply a thin layer of glue on the flat base of the glass stone and place on top of the paper. As you push down, remove any excess glue from the edges using a soft, damp cloth. Hold the stone down for a few seconds until you can feel the glue setting.

4. Once the glue is dry, take your scissors and carefully cut around the edge of the paper, cautiously to the edge of the stone.

5. Now you have cut out your paper glass stone, apply a further thin layer of glue to the back of the paper.

6. Then place and push down onto your white felt backing sheet. Utilise the paper and felt sheets wisely by working across from corner to corner, avoiding any wastage.

7. Repeat step 4, and neatly cut around the edge of the stone.

8. Allow 2 hours for the glass stone to dry. The glue will dry faster in a warm, dry room.

9. Now you can repeat the process for each stone in your kit, selecting complimentary areas of the paper to create an abstract rainbow effect on all the glass stones.

10. Once you get to your smaller glass stones, take your time, and enjoy perfecting a neat all-round finish. Treasure your collective glass stones and display them proudly in your home.

NOTES

Use the space below to make your own personal notes on the previous project to help when you come back to make it again!

COLOUR BLOCK

COLOUR BLOCK

Add these trendy glass stones to your jewellery collection they're ideal for that summer outfit!

YOU WILL NEED

·Glass stones
·Nail varnish
·Thin crafting felt
·Craft scissors
·Dry cloth

METHOD

1. Make sure you're working on a clean and spacious work surface; this is all part of the mindfulness and enjoyment of glass stone craft. Once ready, lay out your stones and give each stone a nice wipe over with a soft, dry cloth.

2. Before applying nail varnish, make sure you have a well-ventilated workspace.

3. Here we have selected 4 colours to use on our glass stones.

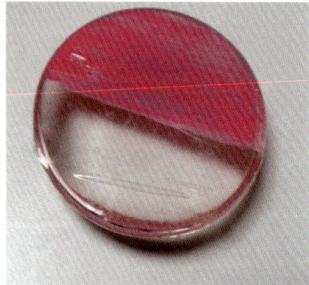

4. Using your main selected colour, brush a section over the bottom half of the flat side of the glass stone.

5. Then, select your next colour and paint a quarter of the stone. Fill the last quarter with another colour. Allow to air-dry.

6. Once dry, apply a thin layer of glue across your colour block art, and place firmly down onto your felt backing.

7. Repeat this process for the other sizes of glass stones, changing up the style of each design.

8. Once dry cut out the glass stones from the felt backing.

NOTES

Use the space below to make your own personal notes on the previous project to help when you come back to make it again!

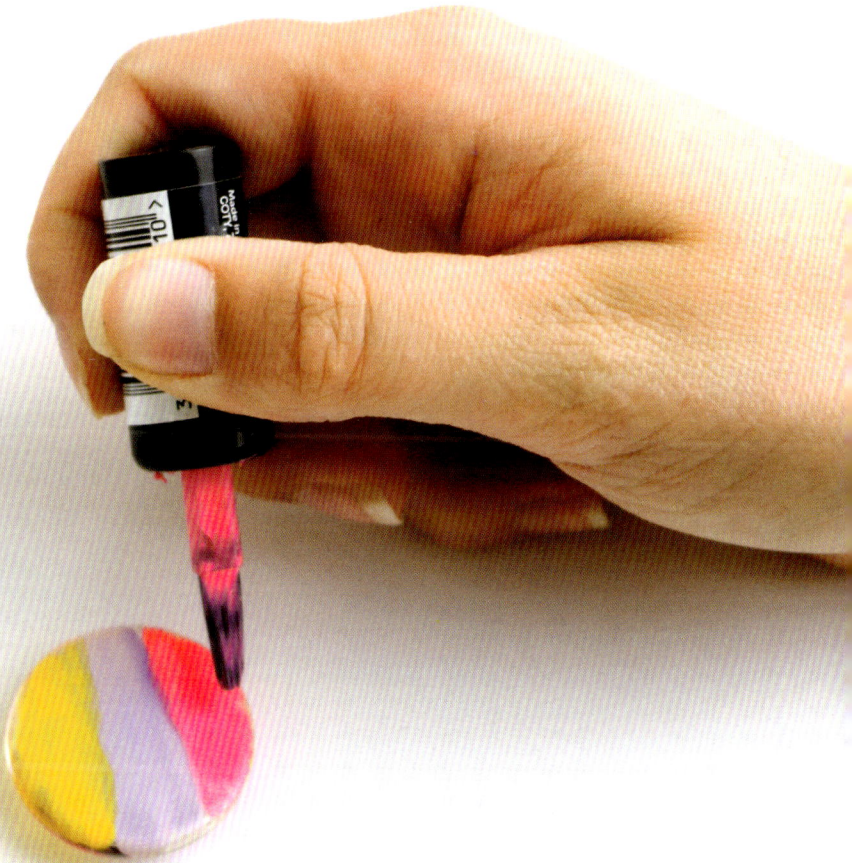

PRESSED FLORAL
MAGNETS

PRESSED FLORALS

Add some colour to your fridge with these wonderful pressed, floral glass stone magnets.

YOU WILL NEED

- Glass stones
- Photographs
- Self adhesive magnetic sheets
- Craft scissors
- Soft cloth
- Pencil or pen
- Ruler

METHOD

1. Make sure you're working on a clean and spacious work surface; this is all part of the mindfulness and enjoyment of glass stone craft. Once ready, lay out your stones and give each stone a nice wipe over with a soft, dry cloth.

2. Photo album at the ready! Alternately, use any photographic imagery. In this case, we have used some lovely photographs of pressed florals.

3. We have measured each stone and created our floral artwork to scale, so they fit within the dome. If you are using existing photographs, you could scan them and re-size the imagery.

4. Once you have your printed images, place the glass stones over the photograph first to make sure they look good.

5. Once happy, brush your glue onto the flat side of stone.

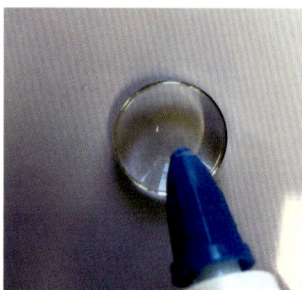

6. Now, place each stone one by one over each image.

7. Once dry, carefully cut around the base of each glass stone.

8. Using your self adhesive magnet sheets, draw around a small glass stone and cut out. Then simply peel the backing off and stick to the base of your glass stone.

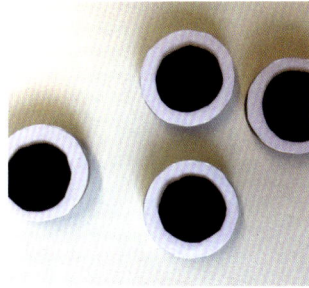

9. Well done! Place these on your fridge or on a magnetic surface.

NOTES

Use the space below to make your own personal notes on the previous project to help when you come back to make it again!

SPARKLE
AND SHINE!

GLITTER GLASS

Sparkle and shine with these decorative glitter glass stones!

YOU WILL NEED

· Glass stones
· Glitter
· Craft glue
· Soft cloth
· Thin crafting felt
· Paint brush (optional)

METHOD

1. Make sure you're working on a clean and spacious work surface; this is all part of the mindfulness and enjoyment of glass stone craft. Once ready, lay out your stones and give each stone a nice wipe over with a soft, dry cloth.

2. Sprinkle a mixture of pink, silver, and blue glitter into a small mound onto a clean surface. You can arrange these separately, or mix them together.

3. Add a thin layer of glue to the base of your glass stone and press firmly onto the glitter. This will give it a good covering. You may have to allow to dry and repeat the process to get a better coverage if required.

4. Once dry, apply a thin layer of glue across your glitter art. Place firmly down onto your felt backing.

5. Once the glue has set, neatly cut the felt around the edge of the stone.

NOTES

Use the space below to make your own personal notes on the previous project to help when you come back to make it again!

SCRATCH GLASS
WALL ART

SCRATCH ART

These 90's styled scratch art glass stones look great as wall art!

YOU WILL NEED

· Glass stones
· Scratch art paper
· Wooden stylus
· Box frame
· Craft glue
· Soft cloth
· Paint brush (optional)

METHOD

1. Make sure you're working on a clean and spacious work surface; this is all part of the mindfulness and enjoyment of glass stone craft. Once ready, lay out your stones and give each stone a nice wipe over with a dry cloth.

2. Using scratch art paper, scratch your design into the paper using a toothpick or a wooden stylus.

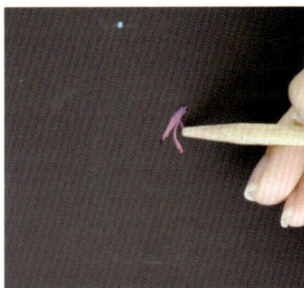

3. Moving the wooden stick in several directions, twist the stick as you go to create different thicknesses.

4. Scratch over existing markings to make some areas appear larger. Experiment with different directions and ways of scratching the art to create an abstract look.

6. Choose the position of your glass stone, apply a thin layer of glue to the flat base and place on top of the paper. Remove any excess glue from the edges as you push down. Hold the stone down for a few seconds until you can feel the glue setting.

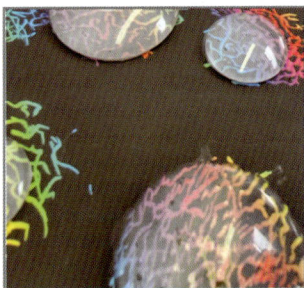

7. Once the glue is dry, take your scissors and carefully cut around the edge of the paper as close to the stone as possible.

8. Once you have your glass stone art cut out and ready, you can then lay your glass stones onto a piece of card. It's now ready to mount into your box frame. Make sure you trim the card to size, ensuring it has a slight overhang to fit on the back of the box frame.

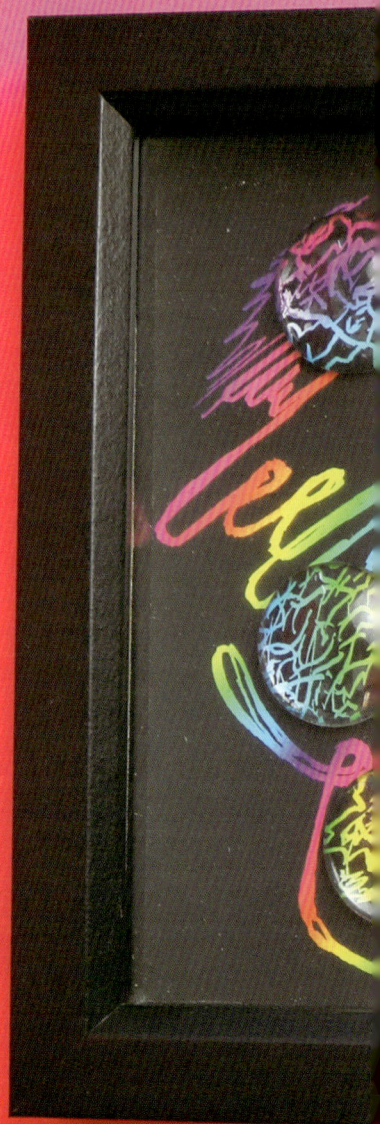

NOTES

Use the space below to make your own personal notes on the previous project to help when you come back to make it again!